Prayer Strategy for Divorce Recovery

by Courtney Hampton-Bennett

All rights reserved. No part of this publication may be reproduced, stored in a retrieval system, or transmitted in any form or by any means-electronic, mechanical, photocopy, recording, or any other except for brief quotations in printed reviews, without the prior permission of the publisher.

Printed in the United States of America.

ISBN: 978-1-953788-05-4

Beyond The Book Media, LLC
5174 McGinnis Ferry Rd. Suite 152
Alpharetta, Georgia 30005

www.beyondthebookmedia.com

Acknowledgments

Special thanks to my mother, Mildred Hampton, and my aunt, Joyce Steele, who encouraged and supported me through my divorce process. From answering my multiple phone calls a day, providing a shoulder to cry on, providing scriptures for me to read, and being by my side every step of the way. I could not have made it through the process or even life without you.

Table of Contents

Introduction 7

Chapter 1 : Forgiveness 10

Chapter 2 : Loneliness 19

Chapter 3 : Depression 28

Chapter 4 : Identifying Unhealthy Behaviors 35

Chapter 5 : Redefine Yourself 41

Chapter 6 : You Are Enough 50

Chapter 7 : Move On & Let it Go 57

Introduction

"In the name of God, I _____, take thee, _____, to be my wedded husband/wife to have and to hold from this day forward, for better, for worse, for richer, for poorer, in sickness and in health, to love and to cherish until we are parted by death. This is my solemn "vow." Those are the vows that my ex-husband and I took on our wedding day surrounded by family and friends with tears rolling down our faces. As a child, I imagined on my wedding day I would wear a beautiful white gown and glass slippers as Cinderella did in the movie. I would walk down the aisle to marry my prince charming. The church would be full of people and beautiful decorations. I would arrive at the church in a horse-driven chariot, greeted by a host of family and friends. My husband and I, on this day, would gaze into each other's eyes, professing our love for one another, and dance all night into the early morning. We would be excited about the new journey we were about to embark upon, for we would no longer be girlfriend and boyfriend but joined together as husband and wife. We would spend the rest of our lives together, have beautiful children, and build our dream home. We would travel the world and be inseparable. Although everything I dreamed of for my wedding day came true, except for the horse-driven chariot and glass slippers, the dream of a lifelong marriage did not. Filing for divorce years later was never a part of the dream.

After seven years of marriage, my fairy tale ended in divorce. I found myself sitting in a lawyer's office fighting back the tears, asking for a divorce from a marriage I had dreamed of since a child. It was hard to build up the courage to file for divorce, but I had no idea what was about to come. The emotional turmoil that I was about to face and would have to overcome to heal was like no other. No fairy tale prepared me for that, and there was no magic wand to make it all go away. It was the most challenging time in my life to overcome, but I did. Although the support of family and friends and their sharing of their divorce stories helped me during this time, it was not until I fell on my knees and prayed to God for help that I experienced true healing. Through consistent prayer, I was able to regain control of my emotions, rediscover the parts of me I had lost, experience healing, move on from memories of the past, and experience peace.

What is recovery without prayer? Prayer is an essential component of the divorce recovery process. It draws you close to God and deepens your relationship with Him. So, no matter the situations you face, you will be able to overcome it.

Sadly, not everyone will have the support of family and friends during divorce recovery, so in addition to prayer, professional help may be needed. There is nothing wrong with seeking help. Never be ashamed to seek professional advice to assist you in your divorce recovery. You are not alone, and mental health professionals can help you cope with divorce and any mental health issues you face.

I also highly recommend that you incorporate the reading of the following scripture Psalms 23 (KJV) into your daily prayer routine during your recovery process. It is a scripture my mother recommended to me that I read daily. It provided me so much comfort and hope.

The Lord is my shepherd (God cares for you and watches over you):

I shall not want (God ensures you have everything you need).

He maketh me to lie down in green pastures (God gives you rest):

He leadeth me beside the still waters (God refreshes your soul).

He restoreth my soul (God heals the parts of you that are wounded):

He leadeth me in the paths of righteousness (God will guide you through every circumstance) *for his name's sake* (According to his will and purpose).

Yea, though I walk through the valley of the shadow of death (In this case, the end of your marriage),

I will fear no evil (God will protect you. Do not worry about what is ahead. Instead rely upon His words and promises): *for thou art with me* (God is faithful); *thy rod and thy staff they comfort me* (God will comfort you in your fear and give you the strength to overcome).

Thou preparest a table before me in the presence of mine enemies (God plans to give you hope and a future): *thou anointest my head with oil* (You are chosen and consecrated); *my cup runneth over* (God will overflow you with blessings, happiness, love, peace, and hope. He will provide you with more than enough).

Surely goodness and mercy shall follow me all the days of my life (God's grace, love, and compassion are always the same from everlasting to everlasting no matter how far from Him you may feel): *and I will dwell in the house of the Lord forever* (You will remain secure in his presence forever).

Chapter 1

Forgiveness

From the Lord's Prayer, "And forgive us our debts, as we also have forgiven our debtors." -Matthew 6:12 (NIV)

"To forgive is to set a prisoner free and discover that the prisoner was you." -Lewis B Smedes

Ms. J wrote as I was sitting in my therapist's office, ranting about how I hated my husband for the things he did to me. My therapist calmly looked up and kindly said, "Ms. J, you are going to have to forgive your husband." "Forgive him?" I said, "There is no way I'm going to forgive the man that cheated on me our entire marriage, that caused our family to fall apart, that manipulated me and took advantage of me. There is no way." The therapist, with a straight face, looked at me and said, "Ms. J; the forgiveness is not for him; it is for you."

It is often difficult to get beyond the painful experience of the divorce and the marriage. Still, forgiveness is the first step to your healing and divorce recovery. Forgiveness involves letting go of all negative emotions, thoughts, or behaviors towards your former spouse and taking a positive approach. You may be asking yourself, how can I possibly forgive someone who has turned my life upside down? How can I forgive someone who has caused me so much pain? Better yet, how can I forgive someone who has caused my children so much pain? Yes, it seems impossible, but with prayer, it can be done, and the process is worth it.

Without forgiveness, you will not be able to get through the journey of emotional healing. Emotional healing not only releases pain but allows profound spiritual growth. Think of it as a way of letting go of your favorite pair of shoes. The ones that are so comfortable but now have holes in it and the sole is coming apart. You want to hold on to them forever, but if you do, all kinds of debris and water will enter through the holes. So, at some point, you know you must let go and replace them with a new pair.

Forgiveness works the same way. At some point in your healing journey, you must let go of the past painful experiences of the marriage and divorce that wore holes in your heart, metaphorically speaking, and caused your soul to fall apart. You must move forward with your life and, in the process, give yourself, your children, and your future new partner the new start they deserve. You must no longer allow those painful experiences to dominate your emotions and cloud your judgment. You must no longer allow unresolved anger, confusion, hurt, resentment, regret, bitterness, or even vengeance to control you. It is written, *"Vengeance is mine, I will repay, says the Lord"* in Romans 12:19. When you allow those emotional strongholds to dominate you, you relinquish control of your happiness to your former spouse and risk making decisions out of anger that you could regret for the rest of your life. You also become victim to those emotions, and set yourself up for emotional bondage, hindering you from moving forward.

Picture yourself carrying a large backpack full of rocks with an additional 50-pound chained rock attached to the outside of the backpack. This load, for many, would be too heavy to carry. This is what happens when you don't forgive. The weight of unforgiveness and emotional baggage over time begins to exceed load carrying capacity and can become one of the heaviest burdens to carry on your life journey. Forgiveness, on the other hand, has the power to release you from that burden. It can give you back your energy and time to focus on more positive things, such as creating new happy memories and reaching your goals.

Forgiveness is not only about forgiving your former spouse; it's also about forgiving yourself. You must forgive yourself for the constant replay of the "If I had not" that took an emotional toll on your mental well-being. For example, the constant replay of "If I had not worked those extra hours or not said it that way or not taken that job or not gained so much weight, maybe my marriage would not have ended." But the truth of the matter is none of those things would have saved your marriage.

When someone loves you, he or she loves everything about you, including your appearance and work habits. That person accepts you for who you are and will never ask you to change; instead, he or she will adapt and push you to be the highest version of you. Therefore, reliving over and over in the mind things you could have done differently will only cause you to be stuck in a vicious cycle of hurtful and depressing thoughts, held in a state of stagnation, unable to find the courage to move forward. And no matter how many times you replay it, it is not going to change the past. Forgiveness also takes away the other person's power over you, allowing you to regain control of your emotions and life. Unforgiveness robs you of the peace that God wants for your life. A peace that will help you move forward.

You must also forgive yourself for the years vested and tireless efforts to keep your family together, for nothing can be more devastating than realizing your efforts and years spent can never be regained. No matter how many years you feel like you wasted, remember it was not a waste. God was with you the whole time, preparing you for greater and, in due season, will bless you abundantly. For God's word says in 1 Peter 5:10, "And after you have suffered a little while, the God of all grace, who has called you to his eternal glory in Christ, will himself restore, confirm, strengthen, and establish you" (ESV).

THE IMPORTANCE OF FORGIVENESS

Forgiveness is a command; and a gift from God that extends grace and mercy. Jesus taught his followers that our forgiveness of others activates God's forgiveness of us. Jesus taught his followers to pray, "Forgive us our debts, as we also have forgiven our debtors." (Matthew 6:12; NIV). Colossians 3:13 (NIV) says, "Bear with each other and forgive one another if any of you has a grievance against someone. Forgive as the Lord forgave you". In Luke 17:4, Jesus says, "And if he trespass against you seven times in a day, and seven times in a day turn again to thee saying, I repent; thou shalt forgive him" (KJV).

Forgiveness extends mercy to the one who hurt you even though they may not deserve it. Luke 6:35-36 (NIV) says, "But love your enemies, do good to them, and lend to them without expecting to get anything back. Then your reward will be great, and you will be children of the Highest because he is kind to the ungrateful and wicked. Be merciful just as your Father is merciful." So, we must forgive to be forgiven. If you refuse to forgive your former spouse of the offenses towards you, by that very act of being unforgiving, God will hold your offenses against you. "For if you forgive others their trespasses, your heavenly Father will also forgive you; but if you do not forgive others, neither will your Father forgive your trespasses" (Matthew 6:14-15; ESV).

The very act of unforgiveness produces arrested development. You become stuck in a place of hurt, confusion, anger, bitterness, and resentment, unable to move forward in your healing. Your wounds remain open and have the potential to become more prominent, even possibly infected. Imagine that you have a cut on your finger. The cut is small, so you just ignore it and go about your day. But after a few days, you notice the cut has gotten bigger, red, swollen, and possibly infected because of the lack of care.

Unforgiveness works the same way, and when you don't forgive, your emotional wounds have the potential to become more significant and possibly infected with hatred and hostility. You must take the time to allow God to work through you and help you get to a place of forgiveness. With forgiveness, you will no longer have to live under the burden of emotional baggage. Emotions that eat away at your physical and mental well-being; and, if not treated, can lead to destructive behaviors. Forgiveness will help you heal and close those emotional wounds. Forgiveness is meant to be the spiritual measure of every relationship, for with whatever measure you measure, it will be measured to you (Matthew 7:2; KJV). Forgiveness opens the door to your healing.

THE MISUNDERSTANDING

Forgiveness is often misunderstood because many individuals believe that to forgive someone is to condone their behavior or to show a sign of weakness. This is so far from the truth. Forgiveness in no way condones bad behaviors or is a sign of weakness. You simply come to a more realistic view of your former spouse. You may have told yourself, repeatedly, that your spouse was going to change or believed that things would one day get better. You may have even blamed yourself for their bad behaviors that contributed to the breakdown of the marriage. However, forgiveness allows you to begin to accept your spouse for who he or she truly is, not the person you created in your mind. Forgiveness allows you to move forward with no more unrealistic expectations.

Forgiveness does not immediately take away the pain nor memories. You can never forget the good or bad memories that you shared with someone you loved. The pain may last for years, but the goal is to get to a place of healing. Most importantly, Jesus teaches us, in the Lord's Prayer, to pray, "And forgive us our debts as we forgive our debtors." Also that "Whenever you stand praying, forgive, if you have anything against anyone, so that your Father also who is in heaven may forgive you your trespasses" (Mark 11:25; ESV). Yes, it may seem unfair, but when you don't try to forgive, you align yourself with the enemy plans for your future. A future robbed of joy, peace, and the life God desires for you.

Forgiveness is also not a quick fix; it is a process. It doesn't happen overnight, and everyone heals differently. For some, it may take only a few months; for others, it may take a few years. Forgiveness is a process that requires a voluntary shift of negative emotions to positive emotions, with an understanding that this shift could cause you to relive painful moments of your divorce or marriage. Moments where wounds may reopen that never truly healed. Moments that you thought were forgotten are now resurfacing. These moments will require you to practice forgiveness over and over. This process will test your patience, strength, willingness to forgive, and willingness to grow spiritually. Know this test will not be easy. In Matthew 18:21-22 (KJV), when Peter came to Jesus, he asked, "Lord, how often will my brother sin against me, and I forgive him? As many as seven times?" Jesus said to him, "I do not say to you seven times, but seventy times seven." Even when you have counted the number of wrongs your former spouse committed and want to say I have forgiven enough, or when your former spouse has shown no signs of change, you still must show forgiveness. Although this process of forgiveness may take some time, it is essential in your walk with God.

STEPS TO ACHIEVING FORGIVENESS

- The first step in forgiveness is learning what forgiveness is.
    - The letting go of all negative emotions, thoughts, or behaviors towards your former spouse and taking a positive approach.
- Learn why forgiveness is so important.
    - Forgiveness is a command by God.
- Read, pray, and meditate on what God's words say about forgiveness.
    - Romans 10:17 (KJV) says, "So then faith cometh by hearing, and hearing by the word of God." It takes a lot of faith to forgive others when they hurt you, more faith then your human will power will sometimes allow. But if you depend on God, you can get through this process.
- Acknowledge your emotions of hurt, anger, bitterness, or regret.
    - The first step towards recovery is acknowledging there is a problem. Also, take time to consider how these emotions are affecting you now. In what ways have they changed you?
- Give yourself permission to forgive.
    - Forgiveness is for you and not so much your former spouse. Forgiveness is a choice. You must decide if you will continue to remain in emotional turmoil or allow yourself to move towards emotional healing, embracing a life free from confusion, regrets, anger, bitterness, and disappointments.

- Forgive yourself and let it go.
    - I know it is easier said than done but not impossible. Forgiving yourself will give you the strength to move on from the past and into a brighter new future.
- Not only pray for yourself but also pray for your former spouse.
    - As Christians, we are called to love each other. In Matthew 5:44 (CEV), Jesus commands us to love our enemies and pray for anyone who mistreats you. So, begin your day with the following prayer.

PRAYER #1

Our Father, who art in heaven, hallowed be Thy name. Thy Kingdom come. Thy will be done on earth, as it is in heaven. Give us this day our daily bread. And forgive us our debts, as we also have forgiven our debtors. And lead us not into temptation, but deliver us from evil. For Thine is the kingdom, the power, and the glory, forever and ever. Amen.

(See Matthew 6:9-13; NIV)

PRAYER #2

Heavenly Father, the creator of all things. Today I choose to set my mind and heart on you. I choose to trust that everything I'm going through right now is working out for my good. I acknowledge that I have resentment, anger, bitterness, unforgiveness, and rage against [former spouse's name]. I confess this is a sin and ask you to forgive me. I also ask that you reveal to me any sins that I need to confess. According to your word and my will, I forgive [former spouse's name]. I release [former spouse's name] and myself from all spiritual and emotional torment. I pronounce the love of God over my former spouse's life that you may fully heal and restore [former spouse's name] as you will me. Lord, you are my strong tower and source of recovery.

Amen.

Chapter 2

Loneliness

Do not be afraid, for I am with you. Do not be discouraged, for I am your God. I will strengthen you and help you. I will hold you up with my victorious right hand. -Isaiah 41:10; NLT

Draw near to God and He will draw near to you. -James 4:8; ESV

Ms. A wrote I felt so alone after my divorce. It had been seven months, and I was so tired of being alone. I was tired of coming home to an empty, quiet house. I was tired of eating alone and hearing my thoughts, not having anyone to talk to. So, I began dating a guy who had been actively seeking a relationship with me for over three months. He would call me every day and voice how badly he wanted to be in a relationship. He would tell me each day how beautiful I was and how much he adored me. He would offer every week to take me to dinner or take me shopping. He would surprise me with flowers or just random gifts to say he was thinking about me. I was so intrigued because not only was I lonely, but he was doing things I had long for my ex-husband to do in the marriage. And, for the first time in years, I felt wanted and beautiful. I felt like this guy was going to be my sunshine after the rain. He owned a business and had his own house. So, I thought well, why not just give the relationship a chance. We would talk on the phone for hours.

We would talk about how we wanted to start a family together, what our children's names would be, things we were going to do together as a family, and the goals we wanted to accomplish. I was so excited to have someone in my life finally, and I fell in love so fast. After a month of dating, I introduced him to my family and friends.

We also decided to move in together. I had never moved so fast in a relationship before, but I was so happy not to be alone anymore that I figured it would be okay. But my fairy tale life soon ended. After three months into the relationship, he became verbally abusive during heated conversations resorting to name-calling. He would also start arguments over the smallest things, such as the method of folding towels. He even threatening to harm me if I even looked at any guy the wrong way. Thankfully, I was able to end the relationship safely, but I feel this would have never happened if I wasn't so eager to find love again and tired of being alone.

Loneliness after divorce is quite common and temporary. After being in a long-term relationship with someone you loved and intended to build a future with, it is difficult not to feel some sense of loneliness. But loneliness does not mean you are alone or considered as something wrong. Loneliness is also not a sign of weakness, nor does it mean you made a mistake; it is merely a part of adapting to change and a new environment. Being in an unhealthy marriage and still feeling alone is much more damaging.

However, for some, the loneliness is overwhelming and terrifying, and the need to find a replacement becomes an act of desperation. The isolation makes you feel as if you are isolated from meaningful relationships. So, you become desperate for the closeness or to feel wanted and needed again. You become desperate to hear someone say I love you, or I'm thinking of you. You become desperate not to continue sleeping in the bed alone. You become desperate not to keep coming to an empty house. You become desperate just to hear someone else talk besides your thoughts. You get tired of seeing everyone else happy, and in a relationship, you become desperate to have someone in your life. So, you set out on a journey prematurely to find love again. Prematurely, because you probably have not done the needed work of healing first before seeking a new relationship.

Loneliness, combined with desperation, can make you vulnerable and susceptible to harm, and, if you are not careful, you can invite the wrong person into your life. A person that God never intended to be in your company. In the letter above, Ms. A describes how her loneliness led her to act in desperation. She was tired of being alone and needed to feel wanted.

Although she allowed someone into her life, whom she thought truly desired a relationship with her, she let him in too soon. She had not given herself time to discover the real character of the man she was allowing into her life. She had not done the work of healing. She had not done the task of developing herself spiritually, for Ms. A was previously married to a man who emotionally abused her for 13 years. He used hurtful emotional tactics such as months of silence, distancing, deflection, and manipulation during their marriage. Healing from the wounds of emotional abuse may take some time, and those who have experienced prolonged psychological damage may have difficulty choosing non-abusive partners.

Completely resolving the past wounds of emotional abuse should be done first before entering any new relationship. Despite Ms. A's eagerness to no longer be alone, no form of abuse is acceptable in any relationship. Abuse is not love. God's word in 1

Corinthians 13:4-7 (NIV) says, "Love is patient, love is kind. It does not envy; it does not boast; it is not proud. It is not rude; it is not self-seeking; it is not easily angered; it keeps no record of wrong. Love does not delight in evil but rejoices with the truth. It always protects, always trusts, always hopes, always preserves. Love never fails."

THE DECEIVER

Loneliness is very deceiving and a significant factor that drives people into unhealthy relationships after recently divorced. Loneliness can lead you to believe that you are unwanted, unloved, undesired, inadequate, insecure, disconnected, broken, and abandoned. It can make you feel discouraged and emotionally frustrated, causing you to lash out at others, not meaning to do so. It can lead you to feel like you are in one of the darkest times of your life, and if prolonged, it can lead to depression.

Loneliness can lead you to believe that you need to be in a relationship to be happy, but happiness starts within. It will have you pushing people away or calling them more than usual, trying to hold on to them because you are alone. Loneliness will have you posting more than usual on social media or saying things on social media you would have never mentioned before for the attention. Loneliness can also take a toll on your physical and mental health, leading to conditions such as alcoholism, memory loss, heart disease, weakened immune system, obesity, malnutrition, or sleep problems.

It is incredible how deceptive loneliness is. It can cause your mind to believe things that are not true, and over time, force your physical body to decline. Gautama Buddha quoted, "What you think, you become. What you feel you attract. What you imagine you create." Your thoughts control you and directly affect your attitude, emotions, behaviors, and actions. Proverbs 23:7 (KJV) says as a man thinketh in his heart, so is he. Meaning what you think is what you become. So, you must bring into captivity every thought to the obedience of Christ (2 Corinthians 10:5; NKJV). Your thoughts can change the course of your life.

By prayer, you must guard your mind for what you allow to enter will flow to your heart and become a part of you. Prayer will help resolve your negative emotions, guard your mind and heart, and give you inner peace and assurance. You can focus on loneliness, isolation, insecurities, or brokenness. Or you can focus on creating a place of peace, love, confidence, and growth. As Joyce Meyers puts it, "You cannot have a positive life and a negative mind." The outcome of your joy, peace, and healing lies in your hand, not your former spouse. You have more control than you think, and no matter how much you feel that you are alone, you are not. God is right there; and, he is faithful. He will never leave you nor forsake you. He loves you more than you know or could comprehend.

THE OPPORTUNITY

Although it may not feel like it, loneliness is a time when positive changes can occur. A time that allows you to draw closer to God. In loneliness, God has the opportunity to gain your attention and speak to you like never before. Consumed with trying to fight for and save the marriage, you may have neglected time praying and talking to God. You may have forgotten that all you needed to do was stay still and allow God to fight your battles. Sometimes God drives people into what seems to be a lonely place to draw them back to him. But you were never alone. God was there the whole time during the marriage. He saw the hurt and pain you experienced. God saw your efforts to save the marriage. He saw all the times you cried. God even heard your prayers. And now, he wants you to redirect your focus to him. Give him all your pain, hurt, and tears. Give him all your plans and desire so you will be able to hear his vision for your life.

God uses loneliness to advance your life. It reveals your weakness and things about you that need to change to strengthen your character. Your insecurities, fears, beliefs, attitude, repressed thoughts, and emotions are revealed to you during loneliness. Loneliness brings forth your real character so that it shines through the darkness. It may not feel good at first, and you may find yourself wanting the isolation to end quickly. In the story of Paul, Paul pleaded with God three times to remove the thorn in his flesh, but God told him His power is made perfect in Paul's weakness. When you are at your weakest, God can make you strong. God's word says that "My grace is sufficient for you, for my power is made perfect in weakness," 2 Corinthians 12:9; NIV. Loneliness is uncomfortable, but over time, it strengthens your patience and faith, for having patience despite the pain is faith. A belief in knowing that in God's timing, everything will work out for your good, and healing is coming.

Loneliness also inspires you to be creative and focus on things you may not have had time to focus on before or perhaps forgotten. Dreams and goals that you set aside for your family. The college degree you always wanted to earn. The business you always dreamed of starting. The trip you always wanted to take. The singing audition you always wanted to try out for. The visions that God can birth through you during this time of loneliness is remarkable. It is during this time; your dreams and destiny may be fulfilled.

STRATEGIES TO OVERCOME LONELINESS

- Recognize and accept that the feeling of loneliness is normal, temporary, and an opportunity for growth. You are not alone, no matter how much you think you are. God is with you, and this too shall pass.

- Shift your negative thoughts to positive thoughts. When the thoughts begin to occur, replace them with positive thinking. For example, if the thought occurs, I'm feeling lonely, replace it with I am not alone, I have friends and family that love me.

- Change the conversation. Focus on the here and now. Have conversations with others that do not focus on the divorce or aspects of the marriage. You cannot change the past. Instead of dwelling on the things you could have done differently or the things that went wrong, focus on how you can move forward.

- Step out of your comfort zone and engage in activities that reduce loneliness. Engage in new activities that will help create new fun memories and reduce your loneliness.

- Reconnect with family or friends. Reach out to someone you've wanted to talk to or visit for a while but may not have had the time. This small act could make a big difference in reducing your feelings of loneliness.

- Find a Hobby. Netflix, over-eating, and sleeping most of the day is not a hobby. Instead, engage in hobbies that you enjoy (e.g., gardening, cooking class, painting, photography, etc.) and hobbies that may also place you in a social gathering. Social interaction with others will help combat loneliness.

- Waste No More Time. Focus on that goal or dream that you always wanted to achieve and formulate a plan to get it accomplished. Now is the time to write that business plan or fill out that school application.

PRAYER

Heavenly Father, I feel so alone right now and lost. My world has been turned upside down, and the life that I once knew has changed. I am starting all over, and most days, I do not know where to start. I often find myself searching for ways and people to fill this void. And even after all the searching, I still fill empty and lost. You have promised that you will never leave me nor forsake me and that you will comfort me in all my trouble. I believe that your word is true. I ask for your comfort and peace during this time. Help me to not dwell on the loneliness and pain that I feel. Help me not to seek solace in man or material things. Help me not to be envious or bitter by lack of love. Help me to focus my mind on you and not the loneliness. Help me to draw closer to you like never before. Help me to conquer this loneliness and all the negative feelings it brings. Mold me into the person that you want me to be and give me the strength to face each new day. Amen.

Chapter 3
Depression

The Lord is close to the brokenhearted and saves those who are crushed in spirit. -Psalm 34:18; NIV

He heals the brokenhearted and binds up their wounds. -Psalm 147:3; NIV

The righteous cry out, and the Lord hears them; he delivers them from all their troubles. -Psalm 34:17; NIV

Ms. E wrote I was married for nine years before filing for divorce. I remember it just like it was yesterday. The day after I filed, I laid in the middle of my cold bedroom floor in the fetal position crying uncontrollably. Begging God to please take my pain away. I couldn't believe my life had gotten to this point. I couldn't believe that I was walking away from the man I loved so much and thanked God for sending into my life. But, two years after being married, my husband changed. He went from being an engaging loving husband to very distant and cold. He began working long hours and was tired all the time. The ringer of his cellphone was always silent, and he would turn his cell phone face down because he didn't want anything to break or fall on the screen, so he said. I would ask him if he was seeing someone else, and he would always deny it. But in my heart, I knew he was.

I just wasn't ready to face it. I also couldn't prove my husband was, so I quickly buried the thought in the back of my mind. Replacing it with thoughts of "Maybe I was just overreacting." I also embedded it in my work. I was consuming myself with work, taking extra shifts, working on projects that consumed most of my time because I didn't want to face the possibility my husband was having an affair. I wanted to believe he was telling me the truth even though his actions said otherwise. After years of his behaviors, not changing, but getting worse, I finally discovered my intuition was right, and my husband was having an affair. The anger and depression I subconsciously hid now surfaced, and it broke me. I didn't want to get out of bed in the mornings, and the only reason I did was because of work and my children. I isolated myself from everyone, including my mother. I was irritable and agitated all the time, verbally mean even to the people I cared about the most. I quit meeting up with my friends as much and dropped many of the activities I enjoyed. Nothing seemed to matter anymore. I didn't care how I physically looked because I didn't have the energy to put in the effort. I couldn't focus on work. I was crying all the time, even during moments I was supposed to be happy. I felt like I was grieving the death of a loved one. I couldn't remember important things like birthdays, meeting dates, etc. I felt like I was losing my mind. I felt like I had lost everything. I was depressed, and I needed help.

The process of divorce is painful and stressful. No one gets married to get a divorce. Also, divorce is one of the hardest decisions to make, and it is also one of the most draining emotionally. The pain of divorce can often feel like you're grieving the death of a loved one, even though no one has passed away. In actuality, you are mourning the end of your marriage. You lost someone close to you, someone you loved, and initially desired to spend the rest of your life with. Divorce is also like being on an emotional roller coaster. One minute you're up and happy. The next minute you're down and crying. You may go from feeling extremely happy to sad to angry in just a matter of minutes. Divorce is a significant life transition that affects not only your life but also the lives of others involved, including children. But, no matter how difficult this period of your life may seem, it is a part of the healing process, and it will get better.

During your divorce recovery, you may experience some or all of the following symptoms of depression:

- Depressed mood most of the day or nearly every day
- Loss of interest in previously pleasurable activities
- Inability to sleep or sleeping more than usual
- Overeating or a lack of appetite
- Agitation or anger
- Fatigue
- Difficulty concentrating, making decisions, or remembering details
- Anxiousness or Restlessness
- Feelings of guilt or worthlessness
- Persistent aches or pain
- Difficulty completing self-care or work-related tasks (i.e., self-grooming, showering, cooking, engaging in meetings)
- Excessive use of alcohol or drugs
- Recurrent thoughts of death or suicide-**Get Help Immediately**

Although some of these symptoms are common during this process, you should consult your doctor or nurse practitioner if you are experiencing any of those symptoms daily and for a prolonged period. Depression is a serious mental health disorder. If you are experiencing recurrent thoughts of death or suicide, seek help immediately by calling your doctor or nurse practitioner, mental health specialist, the National Suicide Prevention Lifeline at 1-800-273-TALK (8255), 911, or your local emergency number.

Do not try to manage these thoughts on your own. Professional help and support can help you overcome the problems contributing to suicidal thinking and identify coping strategies. If you are also relying on drugs or alcohol to manage those symptoms, you need to seek professional help immediately. In the letter above, Ms. E recognized that she was in a state of depression and needed help. There is no shame in asking for help and seeking out support. It is an act of courage, and you deserve a life filled with happiness and love.

COUNT YOUR BLESSINGS

Although it may seem that you lost a lot and your world turned upside down, but you still have a lot to be thankful for. Divorce can often make you feel like you failed in that area of your life, but the marriage wasn't all there was to you or your life. Remember who you were before the marriage. Remember the goals and dreams that you set for yourself. You may no longer be able to achieve the goals and dreams you set for the marriage, but there is still time to complete your own. Now is not the time to give up but to push forward.

Each day count your blessings and try not to focus on your problems or failures. Choose to be happy regardless of your current situation. Find time to enjoy every aspect of your life even, the bad. By shifting your thoughts, you change your perspective and create a more positive environment. So, be thankful for your ability to care for your children. Be grateful for the good and supportive friendships you have. Be thankful for the family members that have stood by your side, the job you love, and the home you have. 1 Thessalonians 5:18 (NIV) says, give thanks in all circumstances, for this is God's will for you in Christ Jesus. Everything will work out for your good, and things will get better.

STRATEGIES TO OVERCOME DEPRESSION

- Seek professional help and stay connected.
    - Support plays an essential role in overcoming depression. Talking with people who can provide a listening ear or advice can help you cope with your emotions. Talking with a therapist can also help you get to the root of your depression.

- Socialize.
    - Spending time with family and friends is a good distraction and can help you cope.

- Stop playing those sad love songs.
    - Songs that remind you of the past can make you feel lonelier and more depressed. Instead, play music that is uplifting, encouraging, and will make you laugh and dance.

- Remove things that bring back sad memories.
    - You will not be able to heal if you continue reliving memories of the past.

- Push yourself to do activities you enjoy.
    - You might be surprised how much better you start to feel.
- Formulate an exercise routine (e.g., walking, swimming, yoga class or aerobics, etc.).
    - Exercise releases dopamine, which boosts your mood and improves your energy level.
- Eat a healthy diet.
    - Depression can often lead to unhealthy eating habits, and it is essential to eat healthy food to prevent adverse health outcomes.
- Daily Journaling.
    - Writing in a journal allows you to express your thoughts without holding back.
- Avoid alcohol and drugs.
    - It will not solve your problems and is an unhealthy method of coping. It also has destructive consequences in the long run.
- Minimize contact with your spouse.
    - Excessive contact can trigger painful memories that can lead to depression symptoms.
- Focus on something other than your divorce or current situation.
    - Invest your time in a goal you always wanted to accomplish. It will help shift your negative thoughts.

PRAYER

Heavenly Father, my heart is burdened with despair, my thoughts are filled with past hurts, my eyes are filled with darkness and tears, and my days are consumed with sadness. I grieve the loss of my marriage. I mourn the hopes and dreams I had planned for the marriage. I grieve the losses that I have faced. I feel angry and sometimes confused, for I do not understand why this is happening to me, but I know you, Heavenly Father, know everything. You came from heaven to give us light and hope for the future. Be my light in this darkness that I face, for in you, there is no darkness. Be my hope in depression, for those who hope in you will renew their strength. Be my strength in my weakness, for those who wait upon you shall renew their strength, they shall mount up with wings like eagles, and shall run and not be weary, and they shall walk and not faint. Restore unto me joy and peace, for the joy of the Lord is my strength. Replace my sadness with joy, my tears with laughter, my anger with forgiveness, and my confusion with clarity. Give me a sense of your presence and closeness and pour into my heart peace that surpasses all understanding. I cry out to you today, for I know in my heart that you alone are my hope and strength. You heal the brokenhearted and bind up their wounds. I cast all my burdens at your feet, for you will sustain me. Help me not to dwell on my troubles or the things that went wrong. Help me not to be ashamed to ask and seek for help. Place the right people in my life that can help me reach my healing. Help me to keep my mind stayed on thee for in your word there is healing. I give you thanks and praise today, for you alone are God. Amen.

Chapter 4

Identifying Unhealthy Behaviors

For I know the plans I have for you, declares the Lord, plans to prosper you and not to harm you, plans to give you hope and a future. -Jeremiah 29:11; NIV.

Trust in the Lord with all your heart and lean not on your own understanding; in all your ways submit to him, and he will make your paths straight. -Proverbs 3:5-6; NIV.

I will instruct you and teach you in the way you should go; I will counsel you with my loving eye on you. -Psalm 32:8; NIV.

Mr. S wrote my wife and I were married for ten years before our divorce. During the first year of our marriage, I would try to have conversations with my wife about things that were important to me, and I noticed that she was never really listening. I would ask her questions concerning statements I made or ask for her opinions regarding decisions I needed to make, and she would frequently ask me to repeat it or say, "I'm sorry I was not listening." During conversations, she would also, at times, appear to be staring off into space. I would often wonder what she was thinking about because it didn't feel as if she was thinking about anything I said. I felt ignored, and it was heartbreaking. I thought that I was not important to her.

She would also take the advice of others over mine concerning any issues she faced. Over time, I shut down and felt I wasn't important to my wife. I stopped talking and instead just listened when she spoke. I became so withdrawn and started to lose confidence in my abilities as her husband. I began confiding in other people regarding my issues, which also led to a 4-year long affair with another lady. My wife's disconnect did not justify the relationship. I just needed to feel like a man in control again. I just needed to feel needed again.

Identifying unhealthy behaviors you exhibited before and during the divorce is essential in the healing process. To move forward in a new relationship, you must be willing to identify those behaviors and take accountability, so they do not reoccur and sabotage your new relationship. Often, during the divorce process, one spouse will focus on the wrongs of the other, but when both sides of the story are told, unhealthy behaviors were usually displayed on both parts. These behaviors could have ranged from poor communication, addictions (e.g., excessive spending, gambling, food, alcohol, extreme gaming, or use of technology), avoiding intimacy, prioritizing friends and family members before spouse, lack of small gestures, always forgetting essential dates, belittling, name-calling, controlling, and abusive practices. These behaviors are sometimes challenging to identify on your own, and even more challenging to recognize when you are in the peak of the marriage falling apart.

Often after the marriage has ended and you have the time to reflect on things that you realize the things you could have done or said differently. No, this does not mean you were the cause of your marriage falling apart or the reason for the divorce. But if these behaviors are not corrected, they can sabotage future relationships.

Unhealthy behaviors cause conflict within the relationship and with any children involved. These behaviors usually develop over time and can intensify. Therefore, these behaviors must be faced and addressed, so they do not interfere in the relationship with your future partner. Acknowledging or recognizing those behaviors may also require the help of a therapist. Therapists are trained to help you get to the root of your problems and identify the source of unhealthy emotions and behaviors. Addictions are often hard to break and have negative consequences. Therefore, consulting a doctor, addiction specialist, or psychologist for help is vital.

In the letter above, although Mr. E's affair was the ultimate cause of his divorce, his wife's listening skills led to the breakdown of communication in the marriage. Often, when that connection is lost with your partner, all other aspects of the relationship begin to disintegrate. Communication is needed for emotional connection. When communication is not healthy, stress and resentment can occur. The bond once made between you and your partner becomes lost. Your partner will begin to feel as if they are not relevant to you and that you do not care. Poor communication can also cause your partner to shut down and become distant. It may also lead to a shutdown of intimacy. Your partner may seek out other relationships to replace or find that connection with someone else. Or they may begin to spend more time away from home with those who are willing to listen. Poor communication can make one feel abandoned and can have damaging consequences in future relationships.

SELF-ASSESSMENT

If you are unsure if you exhibited any unhealthy behaviors during your marriage, consider the following questions. What actions did your former spouse express to you that caused the divorce? What behaviors did your former spouse express to you during the marriage that contributed to arguments? Did you have a bad temper? Did you not listen well when your former spouse tried to communicate with you? Were you always unavailable for events or moments your former spouse wanted to share with you? Were you emotionally unavailable? Were you ever critical of your spouse? Were you not taking care of your portion of responsibilities? Did you always forget important dates like anniversary or birthdays? Where you not thoughtful in surprising your spouse with flowers or gifts? Were you secretive about your finances or personal life outside of the marriage? Did you not acknowledge your former spouse's efforts in the marriage? Did your former spouse not feel loved or appreciated? It is vital to own your part in the breakdown of the marriage.

STRATEGIES TO UNDUE UNHEALTHY BEHAVIORS

- Seek professional help.
    - Identifying unhealthy behaviors you exhibited before divorce may be hard to do on your own.

- Make a list of the unhealthy behaviors you would like to change and plan to change them.

- Visualize yourself changing.

- Practice Listening.
    - Take time to hear, acknowledge, and engage in conservations.

- Seek professional help for addictions and/or abusive behaviors.

PRAYER #1

Heavenly Father, I kneel before you today, asking for forgiveness of my sins against you, for you are gracious and full of compassion, slow to anger and great in mercy. Even though my sins hurt [former spouse's name], it was you Heavenly Father that I sinned against. I was not a perfect spouse and could have done so many things differently, but at the time, I was so blinded with my selfishness, I couldn't see the damage I was doing. I was not living according to your word. Your word declares that we should love one another as you have loved us and to submit ourselves to one another as unto you. The weight of my sin weighs heavily on my heart, and I know that there is righteousness in me. I come to you and repent of all my sins. I ask that you reveal any sins that I have not realized I committed and that I need to take accountability for. If I confess my sins, you are faithful and just to forgive me of my sins and cleanse me from all unrighteousness. I ask that you create in me a clean heart and renew a right spirit within me. Set me free from the sins and any addictions that tore apart my marriage. Amen.

PRAYER #2

Heavenly Father, the loss of my marriage has been very painful for me, so I find it hard to forgive [former spouse's name]. I know it is your will that I forgive [former spouse's name], but how can I forgive someone who has caused me so much pain.

Please, Heavenly Father, help me to forgive fully and freely so that I may rid myself of anger, bitterness, resentment, and regret so that I may heal and grow past the pain. I cannot do this without you. You promised in your word that your grace is sufficient, and I trust that your grace will bring me to the point of forgiveness. You have forgiven me so many times. Help me to demonstrate the same unconditional love that you have shown me. Heavenly Father, and please forgive me for holding unforgiveness in my heart. Set me free so that I may live in your perfect peace. Amen.

Chapter 5

Redefine Yourself

I can do all things through him who strengthens me.
-Philippian 4:13; ESV.

I have said these things to you, that in me you may have peace. In the world, you will have tribulation. But take heart; I have overcome the world. -John 16:33; ESV.

For my thoughts are not your thoughts, neither are your ways my ways, declares the Lord. - Isaiah 55:8; NIV.

Ms. K wrote I was married for eight years. My marriage started to fall apart after five years. My husband and I were introduced to each other by common friends during my freshman year of college. My husband, at the time, was a sophomore. We were inseparable and fell in love fast. After just one year of dating, I became pregnant with our first son, and we decided to get married. We didn't realize at first the financial strain having a child would place on our relationship. We decided that since he was closer to graduating from college, I would withdraw from college and get a job to support us until he finished. Once he completed college and found a job, I would then go back to complete my degree. But it did not go as planned. After my husband finished college, he had a difficult time finding a job. After months of searching, he decided to take a job at the local grocery store making nine dollars an hour. We could barely keep the lights on. So, my husband decided to go back to college to obtain another degree that would afford him more job opportunities. The plan was that I take on an additional job to cover our financial expenses. He would continue working at the grocery store in the evenings to help defray any other costs, and our parents would help with our child.

After two years, my husband graduated and found a job within two weeks. I was so excited that the sacrifices I made were worth it. So, I thought. After a year, my husband presented me with divorce papers and a long letter appreciating me for what I had done but that he no longer wanted to be married. He explained that he was never happy in the marriage and was ready to move on. I was furious, and for a second thought, maybe it was a joke. There was no way the man that I love and had supported financially was leaving me. I was devastated and felt like I had been manipulated. No way was this happening to me. After he left our home, I was angry with myself. I kept beating myself up, saying, over in my mind, what did I do to deserve this? Did he use me and not love me? What should I have done differently? Why me? I had given up my college dream for him and our family. I had supported him financially. And on top of that, a week after he left, I discovered I was pregnant with our second child.

No one gets married with the expectation of getting a divorce. We often get married with the hope of growing old together. We sign the marriage certificate committing to be there for our spouse through the good and bad, until death. Therefore, we make sacrifices and give up parts of ourselves physically, emotionally, and mentally to meet our spouse's needs. We also give up old habits or selfishness, for that part of you can no longer exist within a thriving marriage. It is often later in the marriage that you discover you gave up more than just those things. Maybe you gave up your identity, goals, and dreams.

Often during the marriage, the spouse, children, and the harmony of the home become the focus. So, dreams and goals get put on hold. Or we become so focused on issues of the marriage that we forget to focus on ourselves. The sacrifices may have caused you to feel as if you lost your identity. It may have created feelings of resentment for giving up parts of yourself and your dreams, especially if the sacrifices were not reciprocated. It doesn't mean you made a mistake in the sacrifices you made for your family. You just now must find a proper balance of not only putting others first but yourself as well. Putting yourself first will not only help you to value yourself again but restructure your life.

To attract and sustain healthy future relationships, you must learn again how to dedicate time and energy to get to know and love you again. You must find healthy ways to move beyond the feelings of loss. Every experience we have in life, whether good or bad, is an opportunity to learn and grow. It is how you choose to learn and grow from the experience that matters. It is how you decide to redefine who you are and what you want out of life that is important.

Divorce is not a loss or failure but a chance for you to live God's purpose and redefine who you are. God sometimes guides us down a different path. A path we did not initially dream of or was prepared for, but we must trust that this path will bring fruitful new beginnings. We must believe that everything will work out for the good of everyone involved. We must also trust that God sometimes allows chapters in our life to close so that a new book with new chapters can be written, a fresh new start. A fresh new beginning so that his will for your life can be done.

Jeremiah 29:11 says, "For I know the plans I have for you, declares the Lord, plans to prosper you and not harm you, plans to give you hope and a future." No matter how bad it may seem, good can also come from divorce. For some, the good may be the children who were born or the friendships that were developed. For others, it may be the happy memories that were made during the marriage. We may not always understand why certain things happen in our lives, but God does, and his plans for you are far greater than you could ever imagine. God promises that if we love and follow him, all things work together for the good of those who love him. We can rest assured that God will make everything alright.

REDEFINING WITH REFLECTION

Redefining yourself requires reflection but not dwelling on the past. Meditation opens the way to personal and emotional growth. It helps you to learn from your experiences, whether good or bad, and grow from them. Rather than trying to block out the past bad experiences, reflection requires that you address them. This method allows you to see how far you have come or how far you must go for healing.

It is often easy to blame the former spouse or even others for the failure of the marriage, but it is not always easy to see your wrongs or shared responsibility in the marriage breakdown. Reflection will require you to take accountability for any of your past mistakes within the marriage or during the divorce process. When you can acknowledge and take responsibility for your past mistakes, you can make peace with those things and change your future.

There is no need to beat yourself up over the things you can no longer change, but instead learn from them. No matter how uncomfortable it may feel when you can face your past, you can change it. In the letter, Mrs. K states because her marriage failed, she continually asked herself, "What did I do to deserve this?" and "What could I have done differently?" Repeatedly beating yourself up over things you can no longer change does not change the past but can adversely affect your mental well-being, health, and future relationships. Some self-criticism is reasonable, but constant repetitive criticism is not; and, it can halt your progression in recovery. Instead of continually asking yourself questions like, "What did I do to deserve this?" and "What could I have done differently?" try repeatedly saying phrases like these:

"I did my best it's time to move on."

"I will do better next time."

"I choose to be happy and let go of the past."

"I forgive my ex for all the hurtful things that were said and done to me."

By transforming your thoughts, you can change your life after divorce. Understanding yourself at a deeper level will also improve your self-awareness. Relearning yourself and examining how your thoughts, actions, and emotions align together is one of the most powerful tools you can use to move on and find peace. When you become more self-aware, you will be more likely to walk away from opportunities or relationships that are not a good fit for you. You will also become more aware of your bad traits or adopted self-told false truths.

Self-awareness will improve your ability to understand those traits and emotions and replace them with healthier ones. Do not expect this to happen immediately as not everyone will attain self-awareness and inner peace overnight. Self-awareness and inner peace for some take some time but are worth the effort. Taking time for inner reflection will help you adjust to the changes in divorce and navigate through daily life easier. You will become more knowledgeable about your strength and weakness. You will be able to communicate more effectively. It will help you to clarify confusing thoughts you have about the marriage. Problem-solving will also become much more natural and effective when you understand the meaning of your experiences; and emotional expressions.

STRATEGIES TO REDEFINE YOURSELF

- Don't allow your emotions to take over.
    - Gaining control of your feelings will help you gain control of your mental health.

- Give yourself permission to get over past mistakes.
    - Follow the advice of Paul "…forgetting those things which are behind and reaching forward to those things which are ahead, I press toward the goal for the prize of the upward call of God in Christ Jesus."

- Let go of the mindset of missed opportunities.
    - Everything happens for a reason, and God always has a plan.

- Practice mindfulness exercises.

- o Mindfulness exercises will help you recognize your emotions and learn how to respond to them in a healthy way.

- Take time for yourself each day.
    - o Each day spend 10 to 30 minutes doing something you enjoy. For example, reading, writing, relaxing, listening to music, or a home spa day. During this time, you can even dedicate 2 to 3 days a week working towards a dream or goal you always wanted to accomplish. Habakkuk 2:2 says, "…Write the vision, and make it plain on tablets, that he may run who reads it (NKJV)". Proverbs 16:3 says to commit to the Lord whatever you do, and your plans will succeed (NLT).

- Exercise.
    - o If you don't have time for a gym membership, take time, and walk each day for 10 to 30 minutes. Ask a friend or family member to walk with you. Walking will help boost your mood and provide you with a lending ear to help you get through this tough time.

- Take a class.
    - o Taking a class can help you meet people with a common interest and provide a distraction from your troubles.

- Consider making a subtle change to your appearance.
    - o Sometimes the emotional roller coaster of divorce can cause you to neglect your appearance. Consider going to a barber or stylist and get a new hair cut or hairstyle. Consider making an appointment with

a face makeup consultant for a fresh new makeup look or treat yourself to a spa day. Maybe even consider buying a couple of new outfits as a fresh new start. You don't have to make drastic changes. Small changes will help make a big difference and can even help motivate you in making a new start.

PRAYER

Heavenly Father, I come before you today, asking for forgiveness. Forgiveness for not giving you my all and putting you first. I focused and fought so hard to save my marriage and keep my family together that I lost myself in the process. Most importantly, I fought a battle that was never mine to start with; it was yours. Refresh my soul and renew a right spirit within me. Help me to love myself again and to find joy within. Joy, the world cannot take away. Be the light in this dark period of my life and keep me from feeling sorrow. Replace my feelings with forgiveness and a thankful heart for the good times [former spouse's name] and I shared. Help me to move from the past hurt into a life filled with joy and peace. Amen.

Chapter 6

You Are Enough

You alone are enough. You have nothing to prove to anybody.
-Maya Angelou

Your beauty should not come from outward adornments, such as elaborate hairstyles and the wearing of gold jewelry or fine clothes. Rather, it should be that of your inner self, the unfading beauty of a gentle and quiet spirit, which is of great worth in God's sight.
-1 Peter 3:3-4; NIV

For all have sinned and fall short of the glory of God.
-Romans 3:23; NIV

Ms. V wrote I was married to my husband for 11 years. Like most married couples, we had our ups and downs. But infidelity is what tore us apart and tore me apart. After three years of marriage, I discovered my husband was having affairs with other women. Yes, I could have left him at that time, but I didn't. I stayed with him hoping that things would get better. I stayed with him, hoping he would change, for the vow we took said for better or for worse. And I figured this was my worse. He would tell me over and over that he was going to change. He would say to me that he loved only me. Over and over, I believed him because I loved him so much. But over and over, he lied. I would always ask him, "Why am I not enough for you" and

"What am I doing wrong." And over and over, he would give the same repetitive reply, "You are enough, and you are doing nothing wrong." But in my mind, I still felt like I was not enough and could not figure out what he was getting from those other relationships that he was not getting from me.

I tried everything to show him; I loved him and regained his attention. I would put extra effort into looking nice when we went out on dates, but he didn't even notice. I would schedule surprise trips for him, and he wouldn't even acknowledge it. The lack of acknowledgment took an emotional toll on me, and over time I became so consumed with the thought of not being enough that I could barely focus each day. I also began to feel like nothing in life mattered anymore, and I started to give up on myself. If my husband, the one I loved more than anything, didn't desire me, I knew no one else would either. I turned to food and excessive shopping for comfort. I began eating to distract myself every time I felt like the thoughts were too much. I would go shopping just to feel some type of happiness. The happiness never lasted long, though. I did this for eight years, a long time. Until one day, while looking in the mirror, I realize I didn't recognize who I was anymore. It was like God opened my eyes that day, like no other day before, to see the path of self-destruction I was headed down. Not only had I lost myself in my marital problems, but I had lost self-control. I had gained well over 50 pounds, and the look of pain was in my eyes. My self-esteem and confidence were gone. My funds had drastically decreased due to my excessive shopping habit. I felt like I was losing control and depressed. And as I stared at myself in the mirror, feeling helpless, I still could not help but ask God, why wasn't I enough?

Divorce is painful, but the feeling of inadequacy can be even more painful and linger on long after the divorce. It is a pain that slowly eats away at your self-esteem and confidence over time, debilitating you, consuming your thoughts, actions, and emotions. It consumes how you see yourself and how you think others see you as well. It consumes your ability to make sound decisions and even focus on the day to day tasks. It causes you to underestimate your strengths and skills. It interferes with your ability to maintain relationships causing you to explore relationships to fill that void or seek relationships that may not be organic but make you feel adequate. It blinds you of your self-worth and can lead to a path of self-destructive behaviors (i.e., overweight, anorexia, drug and alcohol abuse, overspending, etc.); even mental health issues like depression or anxiety. It has the power to interfere with every aspect of your life and must also be examined during your journey of healing.

In the letter above, Ms. E's marital issues led to feelings of inadequacy, which developed over time. She became consumed with the thought of not being enough for her former spouse, which ultimately led to excessive spending, weight gain, loss of her self-esteem, and depression. She even believed that if her former spouse did not want her, then no one else would either. Her feelings of inadequacy affected how she viewed herself and her self-worth. It is understandable how the breakdown of the marriage could have impacted her view of her self-worth, for when you love someone who doesn't return those same feelings, it leaves you stuck in emotional turmoil and confusion that is hard to overcome.

SELF-WORTH

Self-worth is how you value yourself, and if you do not value yourself, others will not. Your self-worth or value should never be placed into someone else hand or allowed to be determined by someone's acceptance of you. When you begin to allow your self-worth to be determined by others, you will find yourself always seeking the approval of others to prove your worth. Your values and morals should never be compromised for the comfort of someone else. You train people how to treat you, and that includes your spouse or any other relationship. If you desire respect, you must not allow disrespect. If you wish to be loved the right way, you must not accept anything less. You may not like every aspect of yourself all the time, but you must learn to love and accept the version of you that God made. When you begin to accept the version of you that God created, you will start to grow and move closer to your healing. You will begin to see that you are, were, and always is enough. Someone else's inability to see the beauty within you and love you the right way will no longer define you. Your mistakes, failures, and flaws will no longer define you. You are in charge of your self-worth. You have the power to choose if you remain stagnated in self-defeating thoughts or take back control of your life.

Whether the feeling of inadequacy develops in response to infidelity or some other martial issue, it is a feeling that must be dealt with during your healing journey. When a marriage doesn't work for whatever reason, it is a devastating experience and can also cause you to be critical of yourself. You may have questioned your ability to love or receive love in the right way. You might have questioned your ability to be a good wife or husband if you grew up in a single-parent home. You might have wondered about your appearance if you were beautiful enough. You may have questioned whether you did something wrong or if you could have done anything different to save the marriage. You may have even replayed moments or arguments in your mind over and over that made you feel like you were not enough.

Regardless of the questions and no matter the cause of your feelings of inadequacy, you should never allow anyone to define or influence your self-worth. Not even your former spouse or future spouse, for when you know your self-worth, you will begin to value yourself and know that you are worthy of true genuine love. You will no longer be defined by your past, your former spouse, or material things. You will no longer need someone's approval or love to make you feel better about yourself. Instead, you will begin to love yourself, whether you are in a relationship or not. You will realize that you deserve only the best, and you will start to accept nothing less. You will surround yourself with people who respect you, love you, value you, and encourage you to be the best you can be. The love of another person will no longer define your worth or you. You will begin to realize that you are fearfully and wonderfully made (Psalm 139:14; NIV). You will not only love yourself but prepare yourself to love your future partner in a healthy way.

STRATEGIES TO OVERCOME FEELINGS OF INADEQUACY

- Surround yourself with people who value you.
    - People who value you help trigger positive thoughts and emotions.

- Change your thoughts.
    - Your beliefs about your self-worth are crucial to improving your confidence and perception of yourself. Avoid negative thoughts and negative self-talk. Speak positively and positive affirmations concerning yourself to change the direction of negative thoughts.

- Build **yourself** up.
    - Don't rely on someone else to do it for you. Building yourself up will help build your self-esteem and create a practice of self-love.
- Focus on the present.
    - Avoid reliving over and over moments of the past that contributed to the decline in your self-esteem.
- Forgive.
    - Forgive yourself, forgive your former spouse, and commit to loving you again no matter what.

PRAYER

Heavenly Father, I thank you today that I am fearfully and wonderfully made. I thank you that through your eyes, I am more than enough. With your help today, I choose to no longer allow myself to feel anything less than enough. I choose to no longer allow my self-worth to be defined by a relationship, others' opinions, or earthly things. I choose to no longer be defined by the world's standard of beauty. It has robbed me of peace and joy in my life and has prevented me from living life to the fullest. Forgive me for placing more importance on the opinion of others. Your word says I am clothed with strength and dignity, and therefore I have no fear of the future. Release me from the bondage of self-doubt and give me victory over it. Help me to see that what I perceive as a weakness is a strength and blessing. Help me to see myself through your eyes and to see the whole beautiful person you created. You do not make mistakes. Help me to value myself and accept who I am. Help me to have confidence in my abilities and compassion for myself. Give me the strength to overcome and see that I am valued. With your help, I choose to embrace and love me again. Amen.

Chapter 7
Move On & Let it Go

I can be changed by what happens to me, but I refuse to be reduced by it. -Maya Angelou

Forget the former things; do not dwell on the past. See, I am doing a new thing! Now it springs up; do you not perceive it? I am making a way in the desert and streams in the wasteland.
-Isaiah 43:18-19; NIV

Mr. J wrote my wife filed for divorce after 18 years. She was no longer happy in the marriage and wanted to start a new life. I had to leave everything behind, including the house we built together, and start all over. It was the hardest and most heart-breaking thing I've ever had to do. As I stood in the middle of the empty apartment, I rented I felt so lost. There was no sound of my children running and playing in the house. There was no sound of the dogs barking. There was no sound of my ex-wife fussing at the children and myself for being late for dinner. The was no sound of the neighbors' children playing in the yard. The sound of quietness was the scariest sound I had ever heard. I felt so alone, and many times wanted to call my ex-wife to ask if I could come back home, but I knew I couldn't. I knew I had to try to move on.

Moving on and letting go, especially after a long-term marriage, is initially quite scary and hard. Not only are you leaving someone you loved, but you may be leaving your home. You may also be leaving behind extended family and friends and losing time with your children. There may also be considerable financial losses, losses of memories, and future marital goals and dreams. But to successfully move on, you must mourn those losses and move on. After a divorce, the goal is not to stay in a place of stagnation or dwell in a life influenced by old baggage and pain, for when you dwell on it, you continually relive the pain and slow down the healing process. A wound cannot correctly heal if it is continuously reopened. The goal is to build a new future free of resentment and anger towards your former spouse. You must come to terms that your life has changed, and guess what? You are still in the driver's seat. You always have control over how you choose to move forward. The outcome of your change will be based solely on you and the steps you take towards healing.

You must be willing to accept the divorce and be grateful for what you have now. It will be one of the most critical steps in moving forward and healing from the loss of the marriage. When you can accept things for what they are, you will be able to move on. Acceptance gives you the freedom and, over time, peace.

We usually don't think about being grateful when we are in a traumatic or negative situation like divorce. But by turning your attention to the positives rather than the negatives, it will provide you with a sense of assurance that in due time happiness and abundance will return. It will also help you to confront feelings of loss and failure, replacing them with hope, for the scripture says to rejoice always, pray continually, give thanks in all circumstances; for this is God's will for you in Christ Jesus (1 Thessalonians 5:16-18; NIV). With gratitude, you will no longer be overwhelmed by the emotions or memories of the past, and you will instead begin to appreciate your experience. Although it will not heal all of the wounds immediately, it will help lessen the pain.

Just remember, moving on and letting go will not be without challenges. Emotional challenges, spiritual, adjusting to the single life, added responsibilities, or loss of support, just to name a few. But those challenges will not last forever, and better days are ahead. Those challenges will only make you stronger if the work is done to heal and grow from them. Because whether you want to or not, moving on and letting go is a step you must take. An action that also applies to every area of your life that does not bring you happiness, peace, and growth. You must let it go. And even if you and your former spouse later decide to give the relationship another try, you cannot go back in the same way you left. You must do the work of healing to become a better version of yourself.

STRATEGIES TO HELP YOU MOVE ON & LET GO:

- Do not rush into another relationship.
    - Do not look for someone else to fill this void in your life. It will fail. You should be comfortable spending time alone before investing time in another relationship.
- Take some time to grieve.
    - Grieving is a process that must be completed to move forward.
- Ask for help.
    - Don't be afraid. A mental health professional can help you work through your emotions and feelings in a healthy way.

- Learn from your experiences.
    - Learning will help you set boundaries and prevent you from making the same mistakes again in future relationships.
- Embrace change.
    - Not all change is bad and is critical for growth.
- In all situations, be grateful.

PRAYER

Heavenly Father, moving on after divorce has been hard, challenging, and one of the scariest moments of my life. It has taken a toll on me emotionally and financially. It has caused me so much grief and pain. But your word promises that all things work together for the good of those who love you. So, I trust that your will for my life will be done, and blessings are to come. What I have failed to understand, you already know. The path that seems unclear to me, you have already paved the way. Thank you for the memories we made during the marriage. Thank you for the joy of our wedding day, the family we created, and the friends we made. I rest assured in knowing that the divine purpose of our lives was not lost and what we see as an end is the only the beginning in your eyes. Use [former spouse's name] and I to be a vessel for you and help other couples who may be facing the same situations as we see hope in what may feel like a tragedy or loss. Let them also surrender their hearts to you and know that they are never alone. I praise you for your faithfulness and thank you, God, for your goodness and mercy that is new each day. I am thankful for knowing that we never suffer in vain when we follow you, and there will be joy again.
Amen.